FROM MANAGING TO CONQUERING AGORAPHOBIA

Expert Guide To Understanding Agoraphobia Causes, Symptoms, Preventing, Treatment For Optimal Wellness

DR. DASHIELL DANIEL

Disclaimer

This book, is intended to provide information and guidance on the subject matter and is not a substitute for professional medical advice, diagnosis, or treatment.

The author, is not a medical professional, and the content presented here is based on research, general knowledge, and expert guidance available at the time of writing.

The information in this book is provided with the understanding that the author and the publisher are not engaged in rendering medical, legal, or other professional services.

Any reliance on the information contained in this book is at the reader's own risk.

While every effort has been made to ensure the accuracy and completeness of the information presented, medical knowledge is constantly evolving, and new research may supersede the content in this book. The author and the publisher make no representations or warranties of any kind, express or implied, about the completeness, accuracy, reliability, suitability, or availability concerning the information, products, services, or related graphics contained in this book.

This book may contain references or mentions of individuals, products, websites, organizations, or other names for informational purposes only.

The author does not own or endorse any such entities mentioned in the book. Any resemblance to actual persons, living or dead, or actual events is purely coincidental.

Readers are encouraged to consult with qualified healthcare professionals for medical advice, diagnosis, and treatment tailored to their specific circumstances.

The author and the publisher disclaim any liability for any loss or risk, personal or otherwise, arising directly or indirectly from the use of the information presented in this book.

By reading this book, the reader acknowledges and agrees to the terms of this disclaimer.

Agoraphobia: A Comprehensive Exploration" is a ground-breaking book that explores the many facets of agoraphobia and offers a thorough analysis of its causes, symptoms, and treatments. The book starts with a thoughtful Introduction that provides background information on agoraphobia and its historical context, setting the stage for the next chapters' in-depth analysis.

The first chapter describes agoraphobia, including its symptoms, diagnostic standards, and the risk factors and complex causes that lead to its development. The second chapter goes over the different types and subtypes of agoraphobia, including Agoraphobia without a History of Panic Disorder and Panic Disorder with Agoraphobia, giving readers a more nuanced understanding of the disorder's range of expressions.

Chapter 3 then explores common triggers and agoraphobic situations, elucidating the complexities of public transportation, open spaces, crowded places, and the experience of being alone. Chapter 4 covers the essential elements of diagnosis and assessment, going into great detail about psychological assessments, clinical interviews, and differential diagnoses.

The book examines several treatment modalities in Chapter 5, including pharmaceuticals (such as antidepressants and anxiety medications), psychotherapies (such as exposure therapy and cognitive-behavioral therapy [CBT]), and complementary and alternative therapies.

In Chapter 6, the emphasis is shifted to living with agoraphobia, explaining coping mechanisms, the value of creating a support network, and the necessary lifestyle modifications. In Chapter 13, readers are taken through the process of conquering agoraphobia, including methods like progressive exposure, cognitive restructuring, and mindfulness.

"Agoraphobia: A Comprehensive Exploration" culminates in a profound exploration of the disorder, offering a rich resource for individuals, practitioners, and researchers seeking a deeper understanding of agoraphobia and its multifaceted dimensions. The penultimate chapter provides advocacy efforts, personal narratives, and inspirational journeys that celebrate progress.

Overview

Agoraphobia is a disorder of anxiety that has a profound effect on a person's day-to-day functioning. This in-depth investigation attempts to clarify several agoraphobia facets, from historical perspectives and definitions to prevalence and statistical considerations.

Recognizing Agoraphobia Definition And Synopsis

Agoraphobia is a psychiatric disorder defined by a severe fear of places or situations from which escape might be difficult or from which help might not be available in the event of a panic attack. People who suffer from agoraphobia frequently experience anxiety about being in public places, crowded areas, open spaces, or enclosed spaces, which causes them to engage in avoidance behaviors. The severity of this fear can interfere with daily functioning and limit an individual's ability to engage in routine activities. Agoraphobia and panic disorder are closely related because people with agoraphobia frequently develop it after experiencing recurrent panic attacks and associate certain environments with the occurrence of these distressing episodes.

Historical Angles

The historical understanding of agoraphobia has changed over time, reflecting shifts in societal perceptions and advances in psychiatric knowledge. The word "agoraphobia" itself comes from Greek, where "agora" refers to a marketplace or assembly place. Early conceptualizations of agoraphobia often stressed a fear of public spaces, but modern perspectives acknowledge its broader manifestations. Sigmund Freud added to the understanding of agoraphobia by emphasizing the role of unresolved psychological conflicts and unconscious processes. As time went on, psychological theories were supplemented by neurobiological research, offering a more nuanced understanding of the complex interactions between genetics, brain function, and environmental factors in the development of a

Statistics And Prevalence

Understanding the prevalence of agoraphobia is crucial to comprehending its impact on public health. Epidemiological studies reveal that agoraphobia frequently coexists with other anxiety disorders, such as panic disorder or social anxiety disorder. Estimates of the lifetime prevalence of agoraphobia vary across populations and cultures, with estimates ranging from 1% to 7%.

Women are reported to be more susceptible than men, and the condition typically manifests in late adolescence or early adulthood. The burden of agoraphobia extends beyond the individual, affecting family dynamics and socioeconomic aspects.

agoraphobia is a complex anxiety disorder that is typified by an unreasonable fear of circumstances from which escape may be difficult. Examining its definition, historical development, and incidence offers a thorough grasp of the intricacies involved in this condition. In the future, more research and public awareness campaigns will be essential to creating focused interventions and support networks for sufferers of agoraphobia.

CHAPTER ONE
THE NATURE OF AGORAPHOBIA

Agoraphobia is a type of anxiety disorder that is typified by a severe fear and avoidance of situations or places where escape may be difficult or where help might not be available in the event of a panic attack or other incapacitating episode. People who suffer from agoraphobia frequently feel extremely anxious when they are in open spaces, crowded areas, or places where they believe it may be difficult to leave. This fear is not just a preference for solitude; rather, it is a complex manifestation of anxiety that severely limits daily functioning and quality of life.

Signs And Diagnostic Standards

The Diagnostic and Statistical Manual of Mental Disorders (DSM-5) lists the following situations as the diagnostic criteria for agoraphobia: using public transportation, being in open spaces, being in enclosed spaces, standing in line or a crowd, and being outside the home alone. It is important to note that these fears cannot be better explained by another mental disorder, and the symptoms must significantly impair various aspects of life.

Physical symptoms, such as sweating, trembling, increased heart rate, and shortness of breath, frequently accompany the anxiety. Knowledge of these criteria is crucial for an accurate diagnosis and efficient treatment planning.

Reasons And Danger Elements

The etiology of agoraphobia is complex and involves biological, environmental, and psychological factors. In terms of biology, genetic predispositions may be involved, as people with a family history of anxiety disorders are more likely to develop agoraphobia. Neurotransmitter imbalances, specifically those involving serotonin and norepinephrine, are also linked to the development of agoraphobia.

Environmental factors, such as a history of traumatic experiences or a history of being in situations that triggered panic attacks, can also contribute to the onset of agoraphobia. Stressors in daily life and long-term medical conditions may also make people more susceptible to agoraphobia.

Factors Related To Biology

The biological foundations of agoraphobia involve complex interactions between the central nervous system and neurotransmitter systems. Studies have shown that imbalances in neurotransmitters, specifically serotonin and norepinephrine, are involved in the development and maintenance of agoraphobic symptoms. Genetic factors are also important, as research has indicated that anxiety disorders, including agoraphobia, are heritable. Finding specific genetic markers linked to agoraphobia may help develop more targeted interventions. Neuroimaging studies have also provided insights into the neurobiological basis of agoraphobia.

Environmental Elements

A person's history of panic attacks in specific situations can result in a conditioned fear response, which prompts people to avoid those situations to prevent anxiety. Additionally, the societal and cultural context can influence the prevalence and expression of agoraphobia. Societal factors, such as economic instability or political unrest, can contribute to heightened stress levels, potentially increasing the risk of agoraphobia. Cultural norms and expectations can also shape people's perceptions of safety and influence the development of agoraphobic symptoms. In addition, environmental factors play a significant role in the development of agoraphobia.

Psychological Elements

The psychological components of agoraphobia include a variety of behavioral, emotional, and cognitive elements. For example, maladaptive thought patterns, such as overestimating the likelihood of danger or catastrophic thinking, can perpetuate agoraphobic symptoms.

Cognitive processes that exacerbate perceived threats in specific situations are important in determining an individual's response.

Avoidance behaviors, which are the hallmark of agoraphobia, are motivated by the desire to avoid discomfort and avoid panic attacks. Although these behaviors temporarily alleviate the fear, they also reinforce the cycle of avoidance. Finally, intense fear and anxiety are important emotional components of agoraphobia, impacting people's perceptions of safety and threat in a variety of contexts.

In summary, agoraphobia is a crippling anxiety disorder that requires a thorough understanding of its causes, symptoms, and contributing factors to be diagnosed and treated effectively.

Moreover, further research into the underlying mechanisms of agoraphobia will help to improve therapeutic approaches and diagnostic criteria, which will ultimately improve the quality of life for those who suffer from this difficult disorder. Developing targeted interventions that address the multifaceted aspects of agoraphobia will require integrating insights from biological, environmental, and psychological perspectives.

CHAPTER TWO
TYPES AND SUBTYPES OF AGORAPHOBIA

Agoraphobia is a complicated anxiety disorder that is typified by a severe fear and avoidance of places or situations where escape might be difficult or where help might not be available in the event of a panic attack or other incapacitating symptoms. People with agoraphobia frequently lead restricted lives because they avoid different situations that could set off an anxiety attack or other incapacitating symptoms. Agoraphobia can take many different forms, each with unique characteristics and difficulties.

Panic Disorder with Agoraphobia: This subtype of agoraphobia is typified by frequent and unplanned panic attacks; symptoms include intense bouts of anxiety and fear, as well as physical signs like sweating, shaking, and a feeling of impending doom. The fear of experiencing a panic attack can become so great that people begin to avoid places or situations where they fear an attack may occur; this can gradually reduce their comfort zone and negatively impact their everyday activities and overall quality of life. Psychotherapy, medication, and exposure therapy are frequently used in combination to treat Panic Disorder with Agoraphobia patients.

Agoraphobia without a History of Panic Disorder: This subtype of agoraphobia differs from Panic Disorder with Agoraphobia in that it does not always require a history of panic attacks. People with Agoraphobia without a History of Panic Disorder may still experience intense anxiety and fear, but they do not have the characteristic panic attack episodes. The anxiety in these cases is frequently triggered by particular situations or environments, and the fear of not being able to escape or receive help remains a central concern. It can be difficult to diagnose because the fear response may not be as overt as it is in panic attacks. Cognitive-behavioral therapy (CBT) is frequently used in the treatment of this subtype, assisting people in recognizing and altering their negative thought patterns and gradually facing their fears.

Other Specified and Unspecified Agoraphobia: This category encompasses cases of agoraphobia that do not fit precisely into the aforementioned subtypes. Other Specified Agoraphobia refers to situations where the specific nature of the fear does not align with the criteria for the established subtypes but still involves avoidance behaviors related to agoraphobia. Unspecified Agoraphobia is a classification used when the symptoms of agoraphobia are present, but there is insufficient information to categorize the disorder more specifically. These subtypes highlight the heterogeneity of agoraphobia and the challenges in precisely defining and categorizing all cases. Treatment for Other Specified and Unspecified Agoraphobia typically involves a comprehensive assessment to tailor interventions based on the individual's unique experiences and fears. It may include a combination of therapeutic modalities, support groups, and medication, depending on the severity and specific manifestations of the disorder.

The interplay between anxiety, avoidance behaviors, and the impact on an individual's daily life highlights the complexity of agoraphobia as a psychological disorder. Additionally, acknowledging the diversity within agoraphobia subtypes emphasizes the need for individualized and flexible approaches in therapeutic interventions. Knowing the subtleties of these types and subtypes of agoraphobia is essential for accurate diagnosis and effective treatment planning.

CHAPTER THREE
COMMON TRIGGERS AND AGORAPHOBIC SITUATIONS

Agoraphobia is a complex anxiety disorder defined by extreme fear and avoidance of environments or situations that could cause feelings of panic or being trapped. Agoraphobia frequently causes people to limit their activities and can have a significant impact on their daily lives.

When common triggers and agoraphobic situations are examined, it is clear that the fear is not limited to any particular phobia but rather encompasses a variety of scenarios.

This investigation explores the ideas of open spaces, crowded places, public transportation, being alone, and the connection between agoraphobia and specific phobias.

When faced with large, open spaces like parks, fields, or open landscapes, people with agoraphobia may experience overwhelming anxiety because these spaces are perceived as unsafe and insecure. The fear of being exposed and unable to escape can lead to avoidance behaviors that severely limit one's ability to engage in outdoor activities. It is important to understand the psychological mechanisms that underlie this fear to develop effective therapeutic interventions that are tailored to the unique challenges faced by people with agoraphobia.

The fear of losing control or not being able to escape in crowded places is a common reason why people avoid places like theaters, shopping malls, and busy city streets. The social aspect of crowded spaces can amplify the fear, contributing to a sense of vulnerability and heightened self-consciousness. One important way to address the multifaceted nature of agoraphobia in crowded places is to take a comprehensive approach that takes into account both the individual's cognitive processes and the external environment.

Because of its inherent qualities of confinement, unpredictability, and dependence on others, public transportation presents a unique challenge for people with agoraphobia. The fear of being stuck in a confined space, like a bus or subway, coupled with the lack of control over the journey, can be extremely overwhelming. As a result, people with agoraphobia frequently avoid public transportation completely, which restricts their mobility and independence. Understanding the subtleties of this fear is crucial to creating interventions that enable people to travel through these spaces with more assurance and less anxiety.

A common trigger for agoraphobia is being alone, which represents the fear of confronting difficult situations in the absence of a familiar support system. People who suffer from agoraphobia may avoid being alone in a variety of settings, including public spaces and homes because being alone can make them feel more vulnerable. It is important to comprehend the complex interactions between agoraphobia and the fear of being alone to develop therapeutic strategies that address both the particular triggers and the underlying mechanisms that contribute to the fear of solitude.

The relationship between specific phobias and agoraphobia is complex; in some cases, individuals with specific phobias may start out avoiding situations that trigger intense fear, gradually extending their avoidance behaviors to a wider range of environments, and ultimately leading to agoraphobia. Understanding the relationship between specific phobias and agoraphobia is important for early intervention and targeted treatment approaches that address the progression of these anxiety disorders. Specific phobias involve intense fear reactions to specific objects or situations, such as heights, animals, or flying.

As a result, open spaces, crowded places, public transportation, being alone, and the relationship between particular phobias and agoraphobia represent distinct aspects of the challenges faced by individuals with this disorder.

By thoroughly comprehending these concepts, researchers, clinicians, and mental health professionals can develop more nuanced and effective interventions to lessen the burden of agoraphobia and improve the quality of life for those affected. In summary, agoraphobia manifests through a diverse array of triggers and situations, each of which adds to the complexity of this anxiety disorder.

CHAPTER FOUR
EVALUATION AND DIAGNOSIS

Agoraphobia is a complex anxiety disorder that requires comprehensive diagnosis and assessment. In clinical psychology, structured or semi-structured interviews are essential for gaining detailed information about an individual's experiences, symptoms, and how these affect daily functioning. In these interviews, clinicians explore the onset, duration, and progression of agoraphobic symptoms as well as any triggering events or traumas that may be linked to the disorder's development. The interpersonal dimension of clinical interviews allows for a nuanced understanding of agoraphobia.

Psychological Evaluations

Anxiety Sensitivity Index and the Agoraphobia Scale are commonly used to measure the degree of agoraphobic avoidance and the fear of anxiety-related sensations.

 Psychological assessments are essential tools in the diagnostic process of agoraphobia. Standardized measures, such as self-report questionnaires and clinician-administered scales, are employed to quantify the severity of agoraphobic symptoms and assess their impact on various domains of life. These assessments not only aid in the diagnosis of agoraphobia but also help in treatment planning by identifying specific areas of impairment. Cognitive assessments may be used to understand the cognitive processes underlying agoraphobic thoughts and behaviors, providing valuable in

Differential Diagnoses

Differential diagnoses involve a thorough evaluation of symptoms, taking into account the context and specific criteria outlined in diagnostic manuals like the DSM-5.

Discriminating features, such as the fear of situations where escape might be difficult or help might not be available, help clinicians pinpoint agoraphobia as opposed to other anxiety disorders. However, careful consideration must be given to comorbidities, as individuals with agoraphobia often experience concurrent conditions like depression or substance use disorders. Differential diagnoses are an essential part of the diagnostic process since they enable clinicians to distinguish agoraphobia from other psychiatric disorders.

Ultimately, the diagnosis and assessment of agoraphobia require a multimodal approach that includes differential diagnoses, clinical interviews, and psychological assessments.

Clinical interviews offer a means of comprehending the subjective experiences and contextual factors that impact the manifestation of agoraphobic symptoms. Psychological assessments, which include standardized measures and cognitive evaluations, provide quantifiable data necessary for diagnostic accuracy and treatment planning. Differential diagnoses, a sophisticated process of discernment, guarantee that agoraphobia is precisely distinguished from other psychiatric disorders, promoting a thorough understanding of the patient's mental health landscape. Ultimately, this integrative approach is crucial in the field of clinical medicine.

CHAPTER FIVE
APPROACHES TO TREATMENT

Agoraphobia is a severe fear of places or situations that could make one feel helpless, embarrassed, or panicked. People with agoraphobia frequently avoid certain environments, which makes it difficult for them to go about their daily lives. This talk will cover a variety of agoraphobia treatment methods, including medication, psychotherapy, and complementary and alternative therapies.

Antidepressants: Selective serotonin reuptake inhibitors (SSRIs) and serotonin-norepinephrine reuptake inhibitors (SNRIs) are two of the most widely used pharmacological treatments for agoraphobia. SSRIs, like fluoxetine and sertraline, act by raising serotonin levels, which may help with anxiety symptoms. SNRIs, like venlafaxine, influence both serotonin and norepinephrine, providing a treatment option for patients who may not respond to SSRIs alone. The gradual onset of action and possible adverse effects should be carefully considered when prescribing these drugs.

Anti-anxiety Drugs: Because of their anxiolytic qualities, benzodiazepines are another class of drugs used to treat agoraphobia. However, because of the risk of dependency and withdrawal symptoms, their use is typically restricted to the short term. Drugs such as alprazolam can relieve acute anxiety quickly, but they must be used carefully to avoid abuse. Beta-blockers can also be taken into consideration; they work by preventing the effects of adrenaline from being absorbed.

The choice of drug depends on the patient's unique circumstances, including co-occurring conditions, possible side effects, and response to therapy.

Psychotherapy: Cognitive-Behavioral Therapy (CBT): Based on the idea that thoughts, feelings, and behaviors are interconnected, CBT seeks to recognize and alter maladaptive thought patterns that fuel anxiety. Cognitive restructuring assists people in confronting unreasonable fears, promoting a more adaptive mindset.

Behavioral interventions, like graded exposure, expose people to feared situations gradually, promoting desensitization. Finally, CBT provides people with coping mechanisms, improving their capacity to handle anxiety-inducing situations.

An important part of cognitive behavioral therapy (CBT) is exposure therapy, which involves methodically facing feared situations to teach people that the expected negative outcomes are unlikely to happen. This helps to break the cycle of avoidance that characterizes agoraphobia. Exposure therapy can be carried out in vivo, which involves real-life situations, or imaginably, using guided imagery. The gradual exposure process guarantees that people advance at a rate they can manage, leading to long-lasting therapeutic gains.

Virtual Reality Therapy: Technological advancements have led to the development of novel therapeutic modalities, such as virtual reality therapy for agoraphobia. This method involves simulating real-world scenarios in a safe virtual environment, allowing patients to face and navigate situations they find frightening. It offers a secure and adaptable environment for exposure, allowing therapists to customize scenarios to meet the needs of each patient. Studies have shown that virtual reality therapy can be just as successful as traditional exposure therapy, providing a promising avenue for improving treatment accessibility and engagement.

Complementary and Alternative Therapies: These treatments cover a wide range of techniques that can be used in addition to traditional agoraphobia treatments.

Mindfulness-Based Interventions: Mindfulness, which has its roots in techniques like meditation and focused attention, is effective in managing anxiety.

Mindfulness-based interventions help people develop present-moment awareness, which loosens the hold that anxious thoughts have over them. Programs like mindfulness-based stress reduction (MBSR) and mindfulness-based cognitive therapy (MBCT) are structured and incorporate mindfulness into a therapeutic framework, giving patients tools to manage symptoms associated with anxiety.

Yoga and Relaxation Techniques: The mind-body connection that yoga emphasizes promotes relaxation, which helps with stress reduction. Breathing exercises, progressive muscle relaxation, and guided imagery are complementary techniques that people can incorporate into their daily routines to manage anxiety. Physical activities such as yoga, when combined with relaxation techniques, can help reduce the anxiety symptoms associated with agoraphobia.

Supplements: Passionflower, valerian root, and omega-3 fatty acids have been studied for their possible anxiolytic effects; further research is needed to establish their safety and efficacy in the context of agoraphobia. Some people investigate herbal remedies and nutritional supplements as adjuncts to traditional treatments.

The effectiveness of these interventions varies, and caution is advised due to the potential for interactions with prescribed medications.

To sum up, there are many different approaches to treating agoraphobia, including pharmacological, psychotherapeutic, and complementary approaches. Customizing interventions to meet the needs of each patient and weighing the advantages and disadvantages of each modality are important components of a successful treatment plan. As research on the subject develops, an all-encompassing, integrated approach that incorporates different therapeutic components may be able to improve outcomes for agoraphobics.

CHAPTER SIX
COPING WITH STEREOTYPING

Agoraphobia is an anxiety disorder that is characterized by an overwhelming fear of situations in which escape may be difficult or assistance may not be available.

People with agoraphobia frequently avoid public places and social interactions. Agoraphobia can be a difficult experience that affects many aspects of one's life. People with agoraphobia frequently find that their daily lives are restricted by the overwhelming fear of encountering these situations. This restriction can cause significant emotional distress and impairment in functioning.

Adaptive Techniques

Managing agoraphobia requires a multimodal approach that takes into account both the behavioral and psychological aspects of the disorder.

Cognitive-behavioral therapy (CBT) is frequently the cornerstone of treatment, assisting people in recognizing and challenging illogical thoughts and fears linked to particular situations.

One of the CBT's components is exposure therapy, which progressively exposes people to feared situations in a controlled manner, facilitating the development of coping mechanisms. Mindfulness practices and relaxation exercises can also be included to manage elevated anxiety levels. Medications, such as benzodiazepines or selective serotonin reuptake inhibitors (SSRIs), may be prescribed to treat symptoms, but they should be used with caution due to potential side effects.

Putting Together A Support Network

Support groups, whether in-person or online, provide a platform for individuals with agoraphobia to share their experiences, exchange coping strategies, and gain insights from others facing similar challenges. It is impossible to overstate the importance of having a strong support system when living with agoraphobia. People often benefit from the understanding and encouragement of family and friends who play a crucial role in the recovery process. A supportive environment can foster a sense of security and reassurance, acting as a buffer against the challenges posed by agoraphobia.

Modifications To Lifestyle

A person with agoraphobia must adapt their lifestyle to meet the special needs and challenges posed by the disorder. Although avoiding triggers is a common instinct, it's important to find a balance between managing symptoms and leading a fulfilling life. People with agoraphobia may need to change their daily routines to include activities that they can comfortably pursue within their perceived safe zones.

Gradually exposing themselves to feared situations under the guidance of a therapist helps them to expand these comfort zones over time. Workplace considerations may also need to be taken into account; some people may need accommodations or explore remote work options. Lifestyle modifications also include recreational activities, such as discovering pleasurable and manageable pursuits within the limitations of the condition

In summary, the experience of having agoraphobia necessitates a comprehensive and individualized approach to treatment and support.

Coping mechanisms, such as therapeutic interventions and medication, are essential for handling the psychological aspects of the disorder. Establishing a strong support network, which includes understanding family and friends and attending support groups, is crucial for providing emotional support.

Lifestyle modifications, such as modifying daily routines and exploring fulfilling activities, are invaluable for those attempting to manage the challenges of agoraphobia. Taking these aspects into consideration together results in a more comprehensive and successful approach to addressing the complexities of agoraphobia.

CHAPTER SEVEN
OVERCOMING AGORAPHOBIA

Agoraphobia is a severe fear of circumstances or locations from which escape could be uncomfortable or embarrassing. People with agoraphobia frequently avoid specific environments completely. The treatment of agoraphobia is a multimodal approach that includes behavioral, psychological, and self-help techniques. The goal of this all-encompassing intervention is to gradually lessen avoidance behaviors, challenge negative thought patterns, encourage relaxation, and give people the confidence to take back control of their lives.

Progressive Exposure

A key element of cognitive-behavioral therapy (CBT) for agoraphobia is gradual exposure. In CBT, people are methodically and gradually exposed to feared environments or situations. The process starts with less anxiety-inducing scenarios and moves on to more difficult ones.

Gradual exposure gives people the chance to face their fears safely and teaches them that the threats they anticipate are often exaggerated.

After multiple exposures, people become accustomed to the anxiety, which reduces their fear and avoidance. The therapist works with the patient to develop a customized hierarchy of feared situations, guaranteeing a customized and successful exposure therapy plan.

Restructuring Cognitively

A key component of therapy for agoraphobia is cognitive restructuring, which identifies and modifies maladaptive thought patterns that fuel anxiety. People with agoraphobia frequently hold illogical beliefs about the alleged risks of stepping outside of their comfort zones.

Cognitive restructuring entails confronting and rephrasing these distorted beliefs to replace them with more realistic and balanced perspectives. This process is frequently carried out in conjunction with a therapist and assists people in identifying the cognitive distortions that fuel their anxiety. By adopting a more adaptive and rational mindset, people can reassess the perceived threats associated with agoraphobic situations, thereby lowering anxiety and the impulse to avoid particular locations or situations.

Methods For Mindfulness And Relaxation

By addressing the physiological and emotional aspects of anxiety, mindfulness, and relaxation techniques are essential in the treatment of agoraphobia. Mindfulness, which is based on contemplative traditions, is practicing present-moment awareness without passing judgment. Including mindfulness practices in therapy can help patients become more aware of their thoughts and feelings, which promotes acceptance and lessens reactivity to situations that cause anxiety. Relaxation techniques, like progressive muscle relaxation, guided imagery, and deep breathing, are useful in addressing the physical symptoms of anxiety. These methods encourage a state of relaxation, which counteracts the heightened arousal associated with agoraphobia.

Self-Management Techniques

Self-help strategies support formal therapeutic interventions for agoraphobia by empowering individuals to take an active role in their recovery. They consist of a variety of practical and cognitive tools that people can use on their own to manage their symptoms. Based on the principles of cognitive behavioral therapy (CBT), self-help strategies may involve keeping a journal of thoughts and exposures, setting reasonable goals for gradual exposure, and practicing cognitive restructuring exercises. People can also use self-help resources, like books, online programs, and support groups, to improve their understanding of agoraphobia and gain knowledge from others going through similar situations.

Although self-help strategies are not a replacement for professional guidance, they offer individuals

to overcome agoraphobia, a thorough and customized approach is needed that takes into account the cognitive, behavioral, and emotional components of this crippling disorder.

Cognitive restructuring, gradual exposure, mindfulness, and self-help techniques all come together to create a therapeutic framework that enables people to face their fears, question distorted beliefs, practice mindfulness, and take an active role in their recovery. By incorporating these ideas into a well-thought-out treatment plan, both individuals and clinicians can collaborate to open the door to a life free from the limitations of agoraphobia.

CHAPTER EIGHT
TRIUMPHANT NARRATIVES AND MOTIVATIONAL TRAVELOGUES

Agoraphobia, which is defined as a severe fear of circumstances from which escape could be difficult or embarrassing, can have a big impact on a person's life. People who have overcome agoraphobla have a lot to share, and one important way to do this is through personal narratives, which are first-person accounts of people who have overcome agoraphobia.

These narratives often highlight the journey from the depths of fear and avoidance to eventual triumph over the disorder. By sharing their struggles and victories, people with agoraphobia contribute to the understanding of the condition while encouraging hope and resilience in others who face comparable difficulties.

Advocates And Role Models

Within the field of agoraphobia, role models stand out as pillars of strength and fortitude.

These people, who are frequently public figures or activists, utilize their platforms to promote agoraphobia awareness and destigmatization.

By doing this, role models help to create a society that is more understanding and compassionate by dispelling myths about agoraphobia, highlighting the significance of mental health, and encouraging acceptance. Finally, role models are essential in motivating people who suffer from agoraphobia to seek help and create a supportive atmosphere that is conducive to recovery.

Honoring Advancement

Whether small victories or major turning points, acknowledging and celebrating progress is an important part of the healing process. This idea not only highlights the value of positive reinforcement but also encourages those undergoing treatment. Celebrating progress gives patients a sense of accomplishment, which increases their self-worth and confidence. It also generates a positive feedback loop that motivates them to continue confronting and managing their agoraphobia. Families, communities, and therapists all have a part to play in creating an atmosphere that acknowledges and celebrates the steps taken toward recovery.

SUMMARY

Agoraphobia is an intricate and difficult anxiety disorder that has a significant impact on the lives of those affected. People who have overcome agoraphobia share their inspirational journeys and success stories, which offer priceless insights into the human spirit's resiliency. Personal narratives provide a window into the lived experiences of those who have agoraphobia, fostering empathy and understanding. Role models and advocates work to change societal attitudes by promoting awareness and acceptance of mental health challenges. By celebrating progress, persons with agoraphobia and their support systems actively engage in the healing process, empowering and positive environment for recovery.

Despite its formidable nature, agoraphobia is not insurmountable. By combining personal narratives, role models, and the celebration of progress, a multimodal approach to treating and conquering agoraphobia is created.

By raising awareness, understanding, and providing support, society can help create a more accepting and compassionate environment for those who are struggling with agoraphobia.

As we continue to investigate and comprehend the complexities of mental health, the stories of people who have overcome agoraphobia serve as rays of hope, pointing both the disorder's victims and the larger community toward a road of recovery and comprehension.